Research Lights

Research on Problems of Contemporary India

Dr. Parikshit Barot

H.O.D.
Department of Psychology
Assistant Lecturer (Contractual)
Govt. Arts and Com. College, Jadar, Idar
Sabarkantha, Gujarat (India)

CANADIAN
Academic Publishing

2014

Price : $15

First Edition : 2014

ISBN : 978-1-926488-09-7

ISBN Allotment Agency : Library and Archives Canada (Govt. of Canada)

Published & Printed by
Canadian Academic Publishing
81, Woodlot Crescent,
Etobicoke,
Toronto, Ontario, Canada.
Postal Code- M9W 6T3
Phone- +1 (647) 633 9712
http://www.canadapublish.com

FORWARD

There are best collection of research papers in this book the problems of contemporary India, like status of women, marriage, adjustment, schooling, teaching, parenting, self-confidence, achievement motivation and human development, etc.... Author tries to describe in this book about some research and useful conclusions. Who are interested to do the research, this book is very useful to them for growing their knowledge. I wish to Dr. Parikshit Barot for all the best and I hope that he will writes more and more books in Psychology.

- **Kuldip Sankhala**

(M.A., B.Ed., M.J.M.C.)

Contents

1.   Adjustment: The Art of Married Life   1 – 10

2.   Indian Women's Lifestyle Effects on their Safety   11 – 22

3.   Psychological Challenges for Educational System in Contemporary India   23 – 31

4.   Relationship between Teacher and Student: The Base for Positive Schooling   32 – 40

5.   Self Confidence in Male and Female Teachers and Bank Employees   41 – 51

6.   Achievement Motivation and Human Development   52 – 80

1. Adjustment: The Art of Married Life

Before define marriage one should not neglect the word half marriage to understand explicit meaning of marriage now half marriage itself conditional half and marriage never be a half , so required adjustments which effects to various adjustment lets go through this different adjustments like, spouse adjustment, economical adjustment, marriage life adjustment ,social adjustment and in last consequences of adjustment. Positive adjustment of spouse will result no conflicts it means both have excellent, enrich sentimental & mentally feelings towards both side, it will helpful to regulate and generate economic and social situation which effected in deeply to happiest married life. I would like to focus especially here that not only adjustments make happy but due to adjustments sexual relation will also one of the most important preeminent factor to become happy married life, & sexuality scientific knowledge make colorful life. If adjustments are in positively result will come to happiest married life not to advantageous spouse but cover it total society, and in negative adjustments conflict will come up & turbulent to society as a result spouse divorce is end of married life. Going through this at a glance positive adjustment is an art to make happy married life and poor adjustment makes conflicted life.

Adjustment: The Art of Married Life

From birth, human beings go through a series of transitions that have been referred to variously as "stages, "passages," and "seasons." These terms typically define a specific time period with physical, mental, behavioral or other characteristics that are presumed to characterize, that period. "Adulthood" or "Middle age" is one of them. Middle age is generally considered to extend from age forty to age 60 year. It is an especially difficult time in one's life; adjustment to it is greatly dependent on the foundation laid earlier.. Marriage is a social security for all the individuals, i.e. society through marriage system provides security of needs and cares thereby its existence and prosperity is secured. Marriage is for pleasure, happiness and peace of mind on account of satisfaction through interactions with others, trust, understanding and fulfilling social obligations and enriching personality development. A marriage relationship is a delicate, Kaleidoscopic and complex phenomena. It may be very difficult to disentangle anyone particulars casual element. Besides Marital Satisfaction or dissatisfaction or "Marital Adjustment or Maladjustment," "mid-life-crisis" also have some other thoughts to include: Worries about the future, inability to enjoy leisure time, a feeling that health is deteriorating, a negative evaluation of work life, and stress arising from taking care of the elderly.

Marital Adjustment

Marital adjustment denotes emotional stability, intellectual efficiency and social effectiveness people. Marriage is the key to whole some adjustment involvement and satisfaction. Marriage is our most common life style. One definition of adjustment is adaptation behavior that permits us to meet the demand of the environment. Also defined as a response to stress. The person both husband and wife must learn to live together to share, compromise, accommodate, adjust and plan together. Marriage is more important in society to solve our social, cultural, personal and sexual problems.

Marital adjustment is a life longs process; although in the early days of marriage one has to give serious consideration. As Lasswell (1982) points out, "understanding the individual trait of the spouse is an ongoing process in marriage; because even if two people know each other before or at the time of marriage, there is a possibility that people change during the life cycle. Marital adjustment, therefore, calls for maturity that accepts and understands growth and development in the spouse. If this growth is not experienced and realized fully, death in marital relationship is inevitable. Sinha and Mukerjee (1990) define marital adjustment as, "the state in which there is an overall feeling between husband and wife, of happiness and satisfaction with their marriage and with each other." It, therefore, calls experiencing satisfactory relationship between spouses characterized by mutual concern, care, understanding and acceptance.

Fujihara (1998) did a study on 153 married couples which showed that marital adjustment was significantly correlated with subcategories of social adjustment (1) household adjustment (except the spouse), (2) external family adjustment, (3) work adjustment, (4) social leisure adjustment and (5) general adjustment. Thus, marital adjustment may be a part of social adjustment for women, but the two may be discrete for men. A study, made on 1,609 couples from the Russian Army, found that marital dissatisfaction from husband will cross over to the wife directly, whereas the indirect crossover, when a stressor, such as economic hardship or a negative life event increases the strain of a partner, is mediated the impact of the wife's social undermining behaviour on her husband (Westman, Vinokur, Hamilton & Roziner, 2004).

Landis (1975) cites the following factors in the beginning and development of any love relationship that leads to marriage (a) physical attraction (b) satisfaction of certain personality needs like: someone to understand; to respect the ideals; to appreciate what one wishes to achieve; to understand the moods; to help one make decisions; to stimulate the

4

ambition; to give self confidence; to look at; to appreciate and admire; to back in difficulties; to relieve the loneliness, (c) sharing together the special interests and cares, (d) same life goals. On the bases of the above factors the definition of marital adjustment for the present study includes family adjustment, financial adjustment, social adjustment, recreational adjustment, role distribution and sexual adjustment.

Marriage Make Happy

Marriage is one of the most important institutions affecting people's life and well-being. Marital institutions regulate sexual relations and encourage commitment between spouses. This commitment has positive effects, for instance on spouses' health and their earnings on the labor market. The German Socio-Economic Panel, with data on reported subjective well-being. Spouses expect some benefits from the partner's expressed love, gratitude and recognition as well as from security and material rewards. This is summarized in the protection perspective of marriage. From the protective effects, economists have, in particular, studied the financial benefits of marriage. Marriage provides basic insurance against adverse life events and allows gains from economies of scale and specialization within the family (Becker, 1981). With specialization, one of the spouses has advantageous conditions for human capital accumulation in tasks demanded on the labor market. It is reflected in married people earning higher incomes than single people, taking other factors into consideration and explicitly dealing with the possibility of reverse causation (Chun and Lee, 2001; Korenman and Neumark, 1991 and Loh, 1996). According to this latter view, the marriage income

5

premium would be solely due to men with a higher earnings potential being more likely to find a partner and get married (Nakosteen and Zimmer, 1987).

There is a wide range of benefits from marriage that go beyond increased earnings. These benefits have been studied in psychology, sociology and epidemiology. Researchers in these fields have documented that, compared to single people, married people have better physical and psychological health (e.g. less substance abuse and less depression) and that they live longer. The evidence on the effects on health has been reviewed e.g. in Burman and Margolin (1992) and Ross et al. (1990). Waite and Gallagher (2000) additionally survey evidence on income, health, mortality, children's achievements and sexual satisfaction. survey that is focused on longitudinal evidence is Wilson and Oswald (2002). Recently, there has been an increasing interest in the effect of marriage on people's happiness Married women are happier than unmarried women, and married men are happier than unmarried men. Married women and married men report similar levels of subjective well-being, which means that marriage does not benefit one gender more than the other. Two reasons why marriage contributes to well-being are emphasized (Argyle, 1999): first, marriage provides additional sources of self-esteem, for instance by providing an escape from stress in other parts of one's life, in particular one's job. It is advantageous for one's personal identity to have more than one leg to stand on. Second, married people have a better chance of benefiting from a lasting and supportive intimate relationship, and suffer less from loneliness. Among the not married, persons who cohabit with a partner are significantly happier than those who live alone. But this effect is dependent on the culture one lives in. It turns out that people living together in individualistic societies report higher life satisfaction than single, and sometimes even married, persons.

Why Divorce?

Divorce is a complex event that can be viewed from multiple perspectives. For example, sociological research has focused primarily on structural and life course predictors of marital disruption, such as social class, race, and age at first marriage (Bumpass, Martin,&Sweet, 1991; White, 1991). Psychological research, in contrast, has focused on dimensions of marital interaction, such as conflict management (Gottman, 1994), or on personality characteristics, such as antisocial behavior or chronic negative affect (Leonard&Roberts, 1998). One limitation of these approaches is that neither considers the individual's perceptions about why the divorce occurred. Indeed, when explaining what caused their marriages to end, people appear to give relatively little credence to widely studied factors such as age at marriage or conflict resolution skills. Compared with men, women tend to monitor their relationships more closely, become aware of relationship problems sooner, and are more likely to initiate discussions of relationship problems with their partners (Thompson & Walker, 1991).

In addition to understanding the specific reasons people give for divorcing, it is also important to know whether these reasons are linked with post divorce adjustment. Divorced individuals experience higher levels of depression, lower levels of life satisfaction, and more health problems than married individuals. It is not clear, however, whether people's perceived reasons for divorce are related to post divorce adjustment. Although little research has addressed this issue, Kitson (1992) found that individuals who cited extramarital sex reported especially high levels of subjective distress following marital disruption. Attribution theory (Fletcher & Fincham, 1991; Graham & Folkes, 1990; Weiner, 1986) provides a useful framework for understanding how the perceived causes of divorce might relate to post divorce adjustment. If people attribute the cause of a problem (such as being unemployed) to internal factors (such as one's lack of ability), then they are likely to experience negative views of the self and distressing emotions. However, when attribute the cause of a problem to external factors (such as fluctuations in the economy or bad luck); these negative outcomes are less likely. This principle also may apply to divorce—that is, former spouses may have a more difficult time adjusting to divorce when they make internal rather than external attributions about the cause of marital disruption. In particular, attributing causality to the spouse or to external factors should result in the least distress, and attributing causality to oneself should result in the greatest distress. In general, although attributing the cause of the divorce to internal factors should be associated with poorer adjustment, wanting the divorce more than the spouse should be associated with better adjustment, and individuals who attribute the cause of the divorce to their former spouses and the initiation of the divorce to themselves should have the most positive adjustment of all.

In this article I try to focus of adjustment in reference to marital life and couple adjustment. Finally, conclude that great and positive adjustment makes happy married life and poor adjustment does make conflicted life. So adjustment is the art of married life.

REFERENCES

➢ Albrecht, S. L., Bahr, H. M.,&Goodman, K. L. (1983). *Divorce and remarriage: Problems, adaptations, and adjustments*. Westport, CT: Greenwood.

➢ Becker, G. S. (1991). *A treatise on the family* (enlarged ed.). Cambridge, MA: Harvard University Press.

➢ Bloom, B. L., Niles, R. L.,&Tatcher,A.M. (1985). Sources of marital dissatisfaction among newly separated persons. *Journal of Family Issues, 6*, 359-373.

➢ Goode, W. J. (1956). *Women in divorce*. New York: Free Press.

➢ Gottman, J. M. (1994). *What predicts divorce?* Hillsdale, NJ: Lawrence Erlbaum.

➢ Graham, S.,&Folkes, V. S. (1990). *Attribution theory: Applications to achievement, mental health, and interpersonal conflict*. Hillsdale, NJ: Lawrence Erlbaum.

➢ Gray, J. D., & Silver, R. C. (1990). Opposite sides of the same coin: Former spouses' divergent perspectives in coping with their divorce. *Journal of Personality & Social Psychology, 59*, 1180-1191.

➢ Kitson, G. C. (1992). *Portrait of divorce: Adjustment to marital breakdown*. New York: Guilford.

➤ Kitson, G. C., Babri, K. B., & Roach, M. J. (1985). Who divorces and why: A review. *Journal of Family Issues*, *6*, 255-293.

➤ Roberts, L. J. (2000). Fire and ice in marital communication: Hostile distancing behaviors as predictors of marital distress. *Journal of Marriage & the Family*, *62*, 693-707.

2. Indian Women's Lifestyle Effects on their Safety

Indian culture and lifestyle is always a subject of curiosity for the west. In ancient India, the women enjoyed equal status with men in all fields of life. The Indian woman's position in the society further deteriorated during the medieval period. During the British Raj, many reformers fought for the upliftment of women. Women in India now participate in all activities. Indian women's lifestyle is all time effective for their safety like, At ancient time women very safe because there were visible any body part of women in some limits and social rules. They wear social controlled clothing and made their safety in lifetime. Now, we saw that Indian girls and young women are wearing short and skintight cloths and break their safety. In the past a food classification system that categorized any item as *saatvic, raajsic* or *taamsic* developed in *Ayurveda*. Now, the world of fast food is broken human health. In ancient India women entertained with traditional tools and live delightful life. Present women used modern tools for entertainment and live stressful life. Attitude of women in ancient India were very social and familiar focused. In present modern culture mostly changed attitudes of Indian women. Modern Indian girls and young women's beliefs are very personal and lack of social things.

Indian Women's Lifestyle Effects on their Safety.

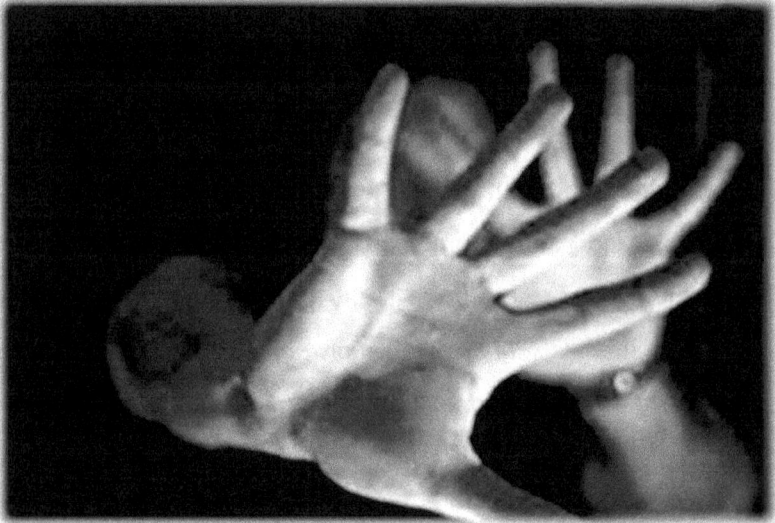

Indian culture and lifestyle is always a subject of curiosity for the west. India, the country of Ten thousand years culture, the land of sharp contrasts and the perfect example of unity among vivid diversity believes in simple living and high thinking. Though Hindu dominated country, peaceful co-existence of people belonging to all religions of the world here is one of the greatest aspects of the Indian culture. Constitutionally, India is a secular country and every Indian enjoys equal rights irrespective of his/her religion, caste, sex and political opinion.

India is credibly the only country with the largest and most diverse mixture of races. A spell-binding country where people of unlike communities and religions live together in oneness. India is a very culturally diverse country. People speak hundreds of different languages (18 major languages, with English and Hindi as the official languages). But the beauty lies in the fact that despite all the differences, people live with full harmony and love depicting their varied cultures, traditions and dressing styles.

Women in Ancient India

Scholars believe that in ancient India, the women enjoyed equal status with men in all fields of life. However, some others hold contrasting views. Works by ancient Indian grammarians such as Patanjali and Katyayana suggest that women were educated in the early Vedic period Rigvedic verses suggest that the women married at a mature age and were probably free to select their husband. Scriptures such as Rig Veda and Upanishads mention several women sages and seers, notably Gargi and Maitreyi.

According to studies, women enjoyed equal status and rights during the early Vedic period. However, later (approximately 500 B.C.), the status of women began to decline with the Smritis (esp. Manusmriti) and with the Islamic invasion of Babur and the Mughal empire and later Christianity curtailing women's freedom and rights.

Women in Medieval Period

The Indian woman's position in the society further deteriorated during the medieval period when Sati among some communities, child marriages and a ban on widow remarriages became part of social life among some communities in India. The Muslim conquest in the Indian subcontinent brought the purdah practice in the Indian society. Among the Rajputs of Rajasthan, the Jauhar was practised. In some parts of India, the Devadasis or the temple women were sexually exploited. Polygamy was widely practised especially among Hindu Kshatriya rulers. In many Muslim families, women were restricted to Zenana areas.

Medieval India was considered the "Dark Ages" for Indian women. Medieval India saw many foreign conquests, which resulted in the decline in women's status. When foreign conquerors like the Mughals and the British invaded India they brought with them their own culture, which in some cases adversely affected the condition of women and in some cases emancipated them.

Over the ages in India women have been treated as the sole property of her father, brother or husband, not been given any choice or freedom of her own. One more reason for the decline in the status of women and their freedom was that original Indians wanted to shield their women folk from the barbarous Muslim invaders. As polygamy was a norm for these invaders they picked up any women they wanted and kept them in their "harems". In order to protect them Indian women started using 'Purdah', (a veil), which covers the body. Due to this reason their freedom also became affected. They were not allowed to move freely and this lead to the further deterioration of their status. These problems related with women resulted in changed mindset of people and they began to consider a girl as misery and a burden, which has to be shielded from the eyes of intruders and needs extra care. Whereas a boy child did not need such extra care and instead will be helpful as an earning hand. Thus a vicious circle started in which women were at the receiving end. All this gave rise to some new evils such as Child Marriage, Sati, Jauhar and restriction on girl education

Indian Women and British Rule

European scholars observed in the 19th century that Hindu women are "naturally chaste" and "more virtuous" than other women. During the British Raj, many reformers such as Raja Ram Mohan Roy, Ishwar Chandra Vidyasagar, and Jyotirao Phule etc. fought for the upliftment of women.

Raja Rammohan Roy's efforts led to the abolition of the Sati practice under Governor-General William Cavendish-Bentinck in 1829. Ishwar Chandra Vidyasagar's crusade for the improvement in condition of widows led to the Widow Remarriage Act of 1856. Many women reformers such as Pandita Ramabai also helped the cause of women upliftment.

In 1917, the first women's delegation met the Secretary of State to demand women's political rights, supported by the Indian National Congress. The All India Women's Education Conference was held in Pune in 1927. In 1929, the Child Marriage Restraint Act was passed, stipulating fourteen as the minimum age of marriage for a girl through the efforts of Mahomed Ali Jinnah.Though Mahatma Gandhi himself married at the age of thirteen, he later urged people to boycott child marriages and called upon the young men to marry the child widows.

Women in Independent India

Women in India now participate in all activities such as education,sports, politics, media, art and culture, service sectors, science and technology, etc. Indira Gandhi, who served as Prime Minister of India for an aggregate period of fifteen years is the world's longest serving woman Prime Minister.

The Constitution of India guarantees to all Indian women equality (Article 14), no discrimination by the State (Article 15(1)), equality of opportunity (Article 16), and equal pay for equal work (Article 39(d)). In addition, it allows special provisions to be made by the State in favour of women and children (Article 15(3)), renounces practices derogatory to the dignity of women (Article 51(A) (e)), and also allows for provisions to be made by the State for securing just and humane conditions of work and for maternity relief. (Article 42).

In 1990s, grants from foreign donor agencies enabled the formation of new women-oriented NGOs. Self-help groups and NGOs such as Self

Employed Women's Association (SEWA) have played a major role in women's rights in India. Many women have emerged as leaders of local movements. For example, Medha Patkar of the Narmada Bachao Andolan.

The Government of India declared 2001 as the Year of Women's Empowerment (*Swashakti*).The National Policy for the Empowerment of Women came was passed in 2001.

In 2006, the case of a Muslim rape victim called Imrana was highlighted in the media. Imrana was raped by her father-in-law. The pronouncement of some Muslim clerics that Imrana should marry her father-in-law led to widespread protests and finally Imrana's father-in-law was given a prison term of 10 years, The verdict was welcomed by many women's groups and the All India Muslim Personal Law Board.

In 2010 March 9, one day after International Women's day, Rajyasabha passed Women's Reservation Bill, ensuring 33% reservation to women in Parliament and state legislative bodies.

Indian Women's Lifestyle Choice

- **Clothing and Safety:**

Traditional Indian clothing for women in the north and east are saris or gaghra cholis and (lehengas) while many south Indian women traditionally wear sari and children wear *pattu pavadai*. Saris made out of silk are considered the most elegant. Mumbai, formerly known as Bombay, is one of India's fashion capitals. In many rural parts of India, traditional clothing is worn. Women wear a sari, a long sheet of colorful cloth, draped over a simple or fancy blouse. Little girls wear a *pavada*. Both are often patterned. Bindi is a part of women's make-up. Indo-western clothing is the fusion of Western and Subcontinental fashion. Churidar, dupatta, Khara Dupatta, gamchha, kurta, mundum neriyathum, sherwani are among other clothes.

At that time women very safe because there were visible any body part of women in some limits and social rules. They wear social controlled clothing and made their safety in lifetime.

Now, the lifestyles and clothing of girls and young women have changed in India.

Western clothing made its foray into the Indian society during the times of the British Raj. Indian professionals opted to wear western clothing due to its relative comfort or due to regulations set then. By the turn of the 21st century, both western and Indian clothing had intermingled creating a unique style of clothing for the typical urban Indian population.

Women's clothing nowadays consists of both formal and casual wear such as gowns, pants, shirts and tops. Traditional Indian clothing such as the *kurti* has been combined with jeans to form part of casual attire. Fashion designers in India have blended several elements of Indian traditional designs into conventional western wear to create a unique style of contemporary Indian fashion. Both miniskirts and shorts are now worn by girls in bigger urban areas.

Now, we saw that Indian girls and young women are wearing short and skintight cloths and break their safety like, skin disorders, breast cancer and to be victim of sexual harassment.

- **Eating and Health:**

Indian cuisine reflects a 5000-year history of various groups and cultures interacting with the subcontinent, leading to diversity of flavours and regional cuisines found in modern-day India. Later British and Portuguese influence added to the already diverse Indian Cuisine.

❖ **Antiquity Foods and Health:**

A normal diet in early India consisted of fruit, vegetables, grain, eggs, dairy products, honey, and sometimes meat. Over time, segments of the population embraced vegetarianism. The advent of Buddhism affected this shift, as well as an equitable climate permitting a variety of fruit, vegetables, and grains to be grown throughout the year. A food classification system that categorized any item as *saatvic, raajsic* or *taamsic* developed in *Ayurveda*. The Bhagavad Gita prescribes certain dietary practices (Chapter 17, Verses 8–10). During this period, consumption of beef became taboo, due to cattle being considered sacred in Hinduism. Many Indians continue to follow this belief, making the use of beef in Indian cuisine somewhat rare. Beef is generally not eaten by upper caste Hindus in India.

❖ **Disadvantages of Fast Food**

Fast food is a trend that is feverishly catching on with our generation. This is mainly because of our fast paced lives in an increasingly competitive society. As the world progresses, everyone gets hard-pressed for time, making a huge population of the modern day families to turn to fast food and ready-made meals. They no longer seem to have time in the day to sit down and cook a meal for themselves and their families. As the name suggests, fast food can be prepared fast and can conveniently be eaten on the run. We can find numerous take-away joints selling hamburgers, pizzas, noodles and fries. Fast food is a relatively new interface in our dietary habits coinciding with the rising popularity of automobiles. It caters to a growing population of mobile individuals who find the convenient and cheap fast food to be an easy recourse. Though fast food is certainly an occasional fun treat, many people tend to have it too often resulting in unhealthy eating habits setting stage for irreversible health disasters for many youngsters. This is because there are a host of disadvantages associated with fast food as they contain high amounts of fats, salt and sugar that affect the health adversely.

- **Entertainment Tools and Relationship:**

    In the ancient India women entertaining with Drama, Classical Dance, Folk Songs, Group Traditional Activity, etc. There were women used these type entertainments and made great face-to-face relationship within them. In present, Indian women's entertainment tools are so modern like, Television, I-pod, Mobile, Internet, Group travelling and all type mass-media, etc and we saw its effects as correspondence relationship, particular behaviour, stressful life, negative thoughts, suicide, etc and live-in-relationship also.

- **Attitudes and Socialization:**

Attitude of women in ancient India were very social and familiar focused. At that time women believed in combined-family and build relationship between similar person and society. There were many women believed in *Black-Faith* and *Strict Social Rules* in medieval period. In present modern culture mostly changed attitudes of Indian women. Modern Indian girls and young women's beliefs are very personal and lack of social things. They believe in broken-family and independent life. So many cases saw that wives wants to live as self-employee and does not want live dependent on their husband's income.

Thus, the researches and the studies conclude that, women's lifestyle effects on their all parts of life and especially to safe life in India. This article also support to the conclusion.

REFERENCES

- "Child marriages targeted in India". *BBC News*. 24 October 2001.
- "Human Development Report; Sustainability and Equity". United Nations Development Programme. 2011. p. 139.
- "Summary of Ctesias' Indica". www.liviticus.org. pp. section 39.
- "The Swadeshi Movement" (Press release). THE RAMAKRISHNA MISSION INSTITUTE OF CULTURE. 2008.
- C. Griffin, "Troubled teens: managing disorders of transition and consumption", Feminist Review,
- Carol S. Coonrod (June 1998). "Chronic Hunger and the Status of Women in India".

- http://indiatoday.intoday.in/story/india-is-fourth-most-dangerous-place-in-the-world-for-women-poll/1/141639.html.

- http://www.culturalindia.net/indian-clothing/sari.html

- http://www.nytimes.com/2012/06/15/world/asia/in-mumbai-a-campaign-against-restroom-injustice.html?pagewanted=all

- http://www.vakilno1.com/bareacts/indianpenalcode

- Jayapalan (2001). *Indian society and social institutions*. Atlantic Publishers & Distri.. p. 145. ISBN 978-81-7156-925-0.

- Ram Ahuja, 1998, *Violence against Women,* Rawat Publication, New Delhi.

- S. Naire, "Economy of emotions and sexual violence against adolescent girls"…, pp. 156-157.vol. 55 (1997), pp. 4-21.

3. Psychological Challenges for Educational System in Contemporary India

The Prime aim of this article is discussion of psychological challenges for educational system in contemporary India. The school behavioral problems considered the most dangerous ones, which face the components of the educational process. Such problems and behaviors could be treated through varying educational programs offered by the school, giving attention to activities, which assuage the school curriculum, expanding communication with parents to understand the economic, social, health and psychological conditions of the students and to promote the social behavior, and to encourage the social life among them in later stages. A large number of students are unhappy and emotionally upset; only a small percent are clinically depressed. A large number of youngsters have trouble behaving in classrooms; only a small percent have attention deficit or a conduct disorder as this review article.

Psychological Challenges for Educational System in Contemporary India

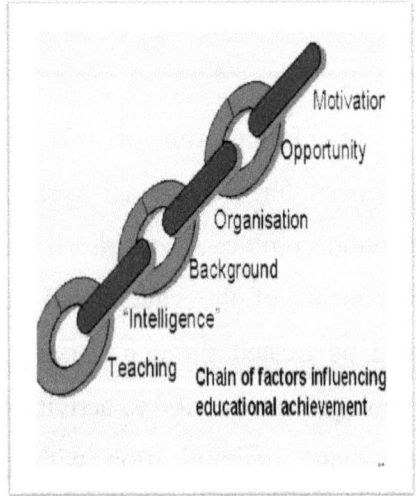

Chain of factors influencing educational achievement

Traditionally, teachers are encouraged to believe that the learning environment must be orderly and quiet. For some principals, a quiet classroom means effective teaching. With the growing movement toward cooperative learning, however, more teachers are using activities in which students take an active role. Sharing ideas and information with various activities occurring at the same time can make for noisy classrooms. But it would be a mistake to conclude that in such classrooms students are not learning (Carr et al. 1998). The classroom management and mastering order inside the classroom are the most important factors in educational process and basic requirements. They are considered the basic problems which face the teacher since teachers complain about mastering the order inside the classroom, and it consumes much effort and time, and they are considered as sensitive, important and critical factors for the teacher's success or failure in his tasks. The concept "classroom order" point to the learner's behavior discipline according to the followed systems and rules which facilitate the process of classroom interaction towards achieving the planned goals (Marei and Mustafa 2009). Glavin (2002) states that the behavioral problems may appear as a result of: inappropriate skills which students learn, choosing inappropriate time for learning, and the restricted learning opportunities offered to students. There are many academic and behavioral problems regarding students that face teacher in the classroom and has a direct impact on the teaching – learning process such as: forgetting school tools, frequent absence, lack of attention, hyperactivity, inappropriate talk in the classroom vandalism, disobedience, aggressiveness, refused to do tasks and school works. There is no instruction without any problems, as long the classroom has different achievement factors, and different personality. The reasons of academic and behavioral problems could be classified as follows (Al-Alga 2006).

School Administration: It plays an essential role in classroom discipline since the dictatorship and unactual laws and instructions of a school administration may push students to challenge those laws and instructions and no commitment with them, which finally reduces the opportunities of discipline and increases the behavioral problems inside the classroom (Al-Khatib 2003)

Teachers: They play a role in the classroom problems when they do not make their objectives clear, and when they do not plan their teaching methods earlier. When teachers follow traditional methods in teaching, this leads to students getting bored, and stressed. This triggers the probability of classroom management problems. A teacher who insists on a classroom full of activity, and quietness' by keeping the students busy, working all the time without any break or any changes in the activities, lead to humiliation working and activity for the students will make the probability of classroom problems due to classroom discipline (Al hajj et al. 2009).

Family: The family lifestyle and environment will put its mark on controlling the behaviors of students. Some students' behavior can be unacceptable at school. Also, the level of behavior that is acceptable and allowed in the family, the way the family acts with one another, leads the student to unacceptable performance in the school. Parents indirectly share in creating problems when they insist on their kids' grades, and achievements to be always high. These lead to feeling of anger, and worry, and create student behavioral problems inside the classroom.

Student's Mental Abilities: Teachers face in the classroom a group of students who suffer from the slowdown, faltering and failure in learning and they need more time than their colleagues need to accomplish any learning task. Such students are characterized by a number of characteristics, including problems of language, oral expression, and unable to pay attention, memory problems and the dispersal of attention (Abu Nemrah 2006). In addition, teachers face another kind of problem in the classroom of gifted students. They are a source of annoyance for the teacher and students in the classroom since they talk without permission, and the ordinary students are always jealous of them (Abu Talib 1996). Finally, such problems and behaviors could be treated through varying educational programs offered by the school, giving attention to activities, which assuage the school curriculum, expanding communication with parents to understand the economic, social, health and psychological conditions of the students and to promote the social behavior, and to encourage the social life among them in later stages. The international disregard of the bad behavior by the teacher and the non- verbal interference through gestures and signals, and approaching riotous students' seats may decrease the behavioral problems.

Owaidat and Hamdi (1997) conducted a study aimed to investigate behavioral problems of the male student in 8th, 9th, and 10th grade in Jordan. The sample consisted of 1907 students from schools identified by educational directorates as having behavioral problems. Students of the sample responded in their class to the questionnaire developed. Data regarding students school achievements were obtain from official records. The result indicates that quarrels, beating other students, cheating in exams and reports, and morning school delay were the most frequently mentioned behavioral problems. The most frequently used procedure to control students was beating by the teacher.

Clunies-Rossel et al. (2008) investigated the relationship between primary school teachers' self-reported and actual use of classroom management strategies. The sample consisted of 97 teachers from primary schools within Melbourne. The information was collected by questionnaire. The findings indicated that teacher self-reports accurately reflect actual practice, that relatively minor forms of student misbehaviors are a common concern for teachers, and that teachers are spending a considerable amount of time on behaviors management issues. Also, the findings revealed that the use of predominantly reactive management strategies has a significant relationship with elevated teacher stress and decreased student on-task behavior.

The study by Leblanc et al. (2008) aimed to investigate the relationship between antisocial behavior during adolescence and high school social climate and a longitudinal and multilevel approach was used. The data was taken from a longitudinal study of 1,233 boys and girls who attended 217 public and private high schools. Students' disruptive behaviors were assessed yearly from 6 to 12 years of age. High school social climate was assessed by teachers, and students reported on their violent and nonviolent antisocial behavior while in high school. The multilevel analyses revealed a large difference between the percentages of variance explained within schools, 97% compared with between schools 3%, teachers' reports of classroom behavior problems explain between school differences in student reported antisocial behavior, after controlling for students' family adversity and history of behavior problems during elementary school.

An extensive literature reports positive outcomes for psychological interventions available to schools. Some benefits have been demonstrated not only for schools, but for society. At the same time, it is clear that school-based applications must be pursued cautiously. With respect to individual treatments, positive evidence generally comes from work done in tightly structured research situations; unfortunately, comparable results are not found when prototype treatments are institutionalized in school and clinic settings. Similarly, most findings on classroom and small group programs come from short-term experimental studies (usually without follow-up). At best, the work accomplished to date provides a menu of promising prevention and corrective practices.

Amelioration of the full continuum of problems requires a comprehensive and integrated programmatic approach. Such an approach may require one or more mental health, physical health, and social services. That is, any one of the problems may require the efforts of several programs, concurrently and over time. This is even more likely to be the case when an individual has more than one problem. And, in any instance where more than one program is indicated, it is evident that inter-venations should be coordinated and, if feasible, integrated.

In children effort to deal with deviant and devious behavior and create safe environments, schools increasingly have adopted social control practices. These include some discipline and classroom management practices that analysts see as "blaming the victim" and modeling behavior that fosters rather than counters development of negative values. To move schools beyond overreliance on punishment and social control strategies, there is ongoing advocacy for social skills training and new agendas for emotional "intelligence" training and character education. Relatedly, there are calls for greater home involvement, with emphasis on enhanced parent responsibility for their children's behavior and learning. More comprehensively, some reformers want to transform schools through creation of an atmosphere of "caring," "cooperative learning," and a "sense of community." Such advocates usually argue for schools that are holistically-oriented and family-centered. They want curricula to enhance values and character, including responsibility (social and moral), integrity, self regulation (self-discipline), and a work ethic and also want schools to foster self-esteem, diverse talents, and emotional well-being.

Thus, this article introduce us for how to affected educational system by psychological challenges and the system how face it, the article also define that how to reduce psychological challenges for educational system in contemporary India.

REFERENCES

- ➤ Clunies-Ross P, Little E, Kienhuis M 2008. Self-reported and actual use of proactive and reactive classroom management strategies and their relationship with teacher stress and student behavior. *Journal of Educational Psychology*, 28(6): 693-710.
- ➤ Colvin G, Sugai G, Patching W 2009. Pre-correction: An instructional strategy for managing predictable behavior problems. *Journal of Intervention in School and Clinic*, 28: 143-150.

➢ Costello, E. J. (1989). Developments in child psychiatric epidemiology. *Journal of the American Academy of Child and Adolescent Psychiatry*, 28, 836-841.

➢ Doll, B. (1996). Prevalence of psychiatric disorders in children and youth: An agenda for advocacy by school psychology. *School Psychology Quarterly, 11*, 20-47.

➢ Wallace, G., & Kauffman, J. M. (1986). *Teaching children with learning and behavior problems.* Columbus, OH: Merrill.

4. Relationship between Teacher and Student: The Base for Positive Schooling

The present paper's prime aim is describes about learning environment through teacher-student relationship. A positive teacher student relationship could be developed by encouraging a learning environment where the student feels free to ask whatever he wants to and the teacher responds in a manner which is understandable by the student. Teachers hold the highest regard for students after their parents. A close, but limited relationship between the student and teacher can be helpful for those students who are shy, and find speaking in front of the classroom difficult or children who have low self-esteem. The relationship between student and teacher, if it is to be maximally productive, must reflect certain attitudes and commitments of each to the other.

Relationship between Teacher and Student: The Base for Positive Schooling.

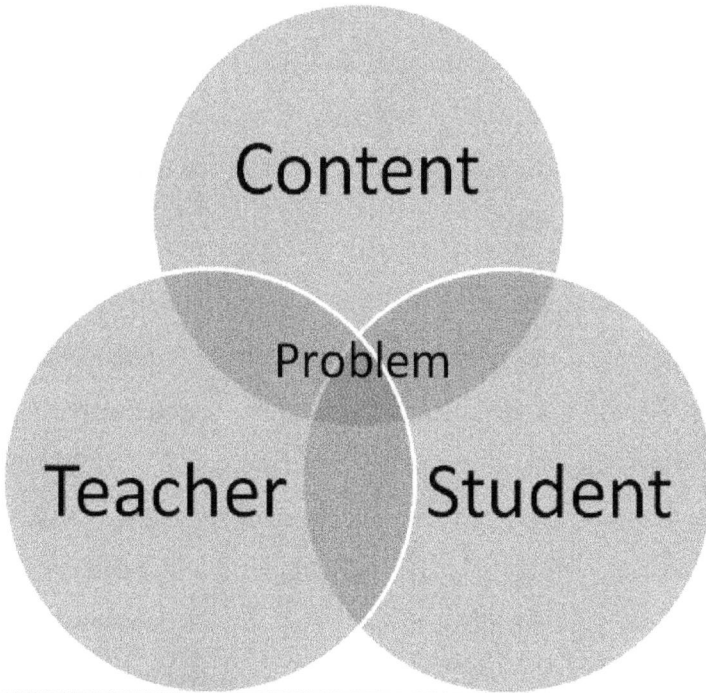

When child first time steps in school's desks, he tries to make relationship with people around him especially the teachers. If teacher start to understand his students there will be a good relationship, because when students have problems on school they can speak freely with their teachers and they can find solution together that is good for everyone. If that relationship and communication student - teacher is good student will have more respect to the teacher and he will pay more attention on his classes. But if that relationship is bad, then going to school and teachers classes will be the biggest nightmare for the student and for the teacher.

Teachers hold the highest regard for students after their parents. All cultures and religions preach that students are supposed to respect their teachers and should try to learn from them not only what's there in the academic curriculum but also the values of life. Teachers have an important role in building the personality of students and the relationship they develop with them determines the student's academic and personal growth.

The teacher student relationship is very important for children. Children spend approximately 5 to 7 hours a day with a teacher for almost 10 months. We ask ourselves what is considered a good teacher. All of us have gone through schooling, and if fortunate had a favorite teacher. A positive relationship between the student and the teacher is difficult to establish, but can be found for both individuals at either end. The qualities for a positive relationship can vary to set a learning experience approachable and inviting the students to learn. A teacher and student who have the qualities of good communications, respect in a classroom, and show interest in teaching from the point of view of the teacher and learning from a student will establish a positive relationship in the classroom. I will be focusing on the relationship between the student and teacher, involving a setting in the primary grades, which I have found second grade to be extremely important for the student to gain a positive attitude for their future education.

Children have different strategies for learning and achieving their goals. A few students in a classroom will grasp and learn quickly, but at the same time there will be those who have to be repeatedly taught using different techniques for the student to be able to understand the lesson. On the other hand, there are those students who fool around and use school as entertainment. Teaching then becomes difficult, especially if there is no proper communication. Yet, teachers, creating a positive relationship with their students, will not necessarily control of all the disruptive students. The book, Responsible Classroom Discipline written by Vernon F. Jones and Louise Jones discuss how to create a learning environment approachable for children in the elementary schools. According to the Jones, "Student disruptions will occur frequently in classes that are poorly organized and managed where students are not provided with appropriate and interesting instructional tasks"

For teachers conducting a classroom and shaping the minds of the young students, teachers who communicate effectively with their students should give appropriate and helpful feedback to their students. Interaction between the student and teacher becomes extremely important for a successful relationship through the entire time of a school year. A close, but limited relationship between the student and teacher can be helpful for those students who are shy, and find speaking in front of the classroom difficult or children who have low self-esteem. The tension these students hold in a classroom will have the confidence they had always wanted, but never achieved due to not having a good relationship with the teacher.

A positive teacher student relationship could be developed by encouraging a learning environment where the student feels free to ask whatever he wants to and the teacher responds in a manner which is understandable by the student. Therefore it would not be wrong to say that the building block of a strong teacher student relationship is effective communication. The level of respect that exists between the two also has a vital role to play in developing a positive teacher student relationship. A major hindrance to the strengthening of their relationship is the different categories of students in a class. Some of the students are hard working and come to the class to learn but there are others who are aggressive in nature and find it difficult to concentrate on what is going on in the class.

Therefore, how does a teacher hold a relationship that leads to effectively teach the children? The answer becomes clear when teachers interact with, and learn more about their students. Our first educational experience, which takes place in the primary years of our life, sets the principles for our future education. Every school year an elementary teacher deals with new faces and new attitudes. Some children find themselves lacking an interest in learning and others feel playing and fooling around at school with friends is the happiest moment of their life. The solution to inappropriate behavior will not automatically get rid of the poor attitude of these children, but is to establish a positive relationship. Teachers can establish a positive relationship with their students by communicating with them and properly providing feedback to them. Respect between teacher and student with both feeling enthusiastic when learning and teaching. Having established a positive relationship with students will encourage students to seek education and be enthusiastic and to be in school. Remembering our favorite teacher will be recognized because they had at least in one way or another the qualities I discussed in this essay, although we are not aware of it during the time we are in school, but teachers are well recognized at a later time of our lives.

Elements of the Student Teacher Relationship.

The relationship between student and teacher, if it is to be maximally productive, must reflect certain attitudes and commitments of each to the other. Specifically, three elements must exist in a student's relationship to a teacher:

First, the student must respect his or her teacher and hold him in the highest esteem, for this is a necessary prerequisite to accepting his advice. Regarding someone who is only giving factual information, and not assuming the role of mentor, this condition becomes less critical. In relation to a spiritual advisor, however, the student needs to feel deference and admiration, for this creates a willingness and desire to receive the teacher's instruction, even though this instruction may be uncomfortable and disconcerting at times.

Secondly, the student must trust the teacher's concern. The student must believe that the teacher always has his or her best interests in mind. If the student would sense some ulterior motive, some self interest, or even carelessness in the teacher's instruction, he or she would not be able to surrender whole heartedly to the teacher's advice, and this would make the entire exchange meaningless.

Finally, the student must commit himself or herself to following the instruction with utmost discipline, for only then can the intended effect be realized. Just as a doctor's orders must be followed precisely, since failure to do so could cause more harm than good, so a teacher's "prescription" must be obeyed with equal conscientiousness and deference to his superior knowledge and authority.

The teacher also has three levels of responsibility to his students in relation to giving advice:

The first is fulfillment of the prerequisite of getting to know his students individually, to probe the innermost depths of their hearts as well as examining the outer details of their lives. As the teacher's familiarity grows, so the potency of his advice deepens proportionately.

Secondly, the teacher must express love and affection toward his students. It is this affection that dissolves the students' natural tendency to resist being told what to do. Thus, the advice can penetrate more deeply and effectively.

Finally, the teacher must take time to reflect upon his students' progress, refining and adjusting his vision of how best to influence them toward positive change. This is an ongoing requirement because students quickly "outgrow" old advice, and the categories of what is beautiful and what is ugly change with each new stage of growth.

The care with which he sifts through various options, seeking that which will satisfy and beautify, is truly an act of love. The measure of a teacher's affection is reflected in his concern for his students' "appearance"--that their personalities be balanced and well proportioned, that they feel at peace with themselves and their environment that they utilize their talents and fulfill their potential. If the teacher's instructions come from such a place of loving endearment, then he will save his students much wasted effort in their journey toward self fulfillment and service of God. In contrast, the advice of a teacher who lacks such particularized concern will be less potent. His cliches and generalizations evidence his own immaturity and narrow mindedness, factors which make his instruction more arbitrary and, necessarily, less penetrating.

This increases the need for teachers to modify their behavior according to each students needs. In this way the teacher would be able to develop a level of understanding with every student and the students would feel they are important which would boost their self esteem. This would also reflect in their grades and overall behavior. The overall size of the class is also vital in determining how effective a student teacher relationship could be. The larger the class size the more difficult it would be for teachers to provide individual attention to students so school administrations should make sure that the class size is kept small which would allow a much better learning environment for teacher student relationship to flourish.

With the growing competition in society it is essential that people improve their relationships with each other. Amongst these relationships, a student teacher relationship is of utmost importance which needs to be looked after properly so that young children could grow up to become educated and responsible citizens of the society.

Thus, present article try to say that relationship between teacher and student must need for positive schooling.

REFERENCES

- Jones, Vernon F., and Louise Jones. Responsible Classroom Discipline. Boston: Allyn and Bacon, Inc., 1981. 95-215.
- Rose, Mike. "Lives on the Boundary." The Presence of Others. Ed. Marilyn Moller. Boston: Bedford/ St. Martin's, 2000. 106-115.
- Thomas, David. "Lives on the Boundary." The Presence of Others. Ed. Marilyn Moller. Boston: Bedford/St. Martin's, 2000. 122.

5. Self Confidence in Male and Female Teachers and Bank Employees

Self-confidence is a feeling which allows individuals to have positive yet realistic views of themselves and their circumstances. The prime aim of the study was to identify and compare the level self confidence in male and female teachers and bank employees. Total 200 professionals were randomly selected from various institutes of Sabarkantha district of Gujarat, out of which 100 were schools teachers and 100 were bank employees from different bank office. The sample was equally divided in regard to gender also. Self Confidence was measured with the help of Agnihotri's Self-Confidence Inventory developed by Dr. Rekha Gupta. Mean scores were computed and 't' test was applied to find out the differences between the groups. The results reveal that the bank employees are more self confident than teachers and differences between the groups find statistically significant at 0.01 level (t=9.88). Simultaneously the male reported high self confidence in compare to female (t=4.88, p<0.01) and furthermore the male bank employees are more self-confident than male teachers (t=7.46, p<0.01), female bank employees have more self confidence than female teachers (t=6.48, p<0.01). Like that male are more self confident than female and bank employee have more self confidence than teachers.

Self Confidence in Male and Female Teachers and Bank Employees

Factors that influence an individual's self confidence and academic performance include the college environment, teachers, peers, and the hidden curriculum, as well as demographic factors such as parents' background affect learners self confidence as well as performance. Self-confidence is our view on our own abilities to do something. The level of self-confidence is usually a result of overcoming certain obstacles or working to improve a skill. Self confidence also refers to a person's perceived ability to tackle situations successfully without leaning on others and to have a positive self-evaluation. Giving the meaning of self confidence Basavanna (1975) states that 'in general terms, self confidence refers to an individual's perceived ability to act effectively in a situation to overcome obstacles and to get thing go all right'.

The personality pattern is a unified multidimensional structure in which the concept of self is the core or center of gravity (Breckenridge and Vincent, 1965). Self confidence is one such personality trait. Dr. John M. Oldham (1995) has defined the Self-Confident personality style. The following nine characteristic traits and behaviors are listed in his The New Personality Self-Portrait.

(I) **Self-regard**: Self-Confident individuals believe in themselves and in their abilities. They have no doubt that they are unique and special and that there is a reason for their being on this planet.

(II) **The red carpet**. They expect others to treat them well at all times.

(III) **Ambition.** Self-Confident people are unabashedly open about their aspirations and possibilities.

(IV) **Politics**. They are able to take advantage of the strengths and abilities of other people in order to achieve their goals, and they are shrewd in their dealings with others.

(V) **Competition.** They are able competitors, they love getting to the top, and they enjoy staying there.

(VI) **Stature**. They identify with people of high rank and status.

(VII) **Dreams.** Self-Confident individuals are able to visualize themselves as the hero, the star, the best in their role, or the most accomplished in their field.

(VIII) **Self-awareness.** These individuals have a keen awareness of their thoughts and feelings and their overall inner state of being.

(IX) **Poise** People with the Self-Confident personality style accept compliments, praise, and admiration gracefully and with self-possession.

43

Self-confidence is one of the most admired attitudes in a person. Employers want self-confident employees because they usually get the work done even in tight situations. Parents hope their children grow up as self-confident individuals. A self-confident person generally has many friends as they are easy and fun to get along with. Alfert (1967) has obtained definite clusters of personality dimensions as self confidence, introversion, extroversion, dominance, sociability, impulse control.

The prime aim of the present investigation is to identify the level of self confidence of male and female teachers and bank employees among sabarkantha of north Gujarat.

Objectives of the Study

The present investigation was carried out to accomplish following objectives.

- To identify and compare the level of self confidence in teachers and bank employees.
- To identify and compare the level of self confidence in male teachers and bank employees.
- To identify and compare the level of self confidence in female teachers and bank employees.

Null-Hypotheses:

- There is no significant difference between teachers and bank employees in level of self confidence.

- There is no significant difference between male and female in level of self confidence.

- There is no significant difference between male teachers and male bank employees in level of self confidence.

- There is no significant difference between female teachers and female bank employees in level of self confidence.

- There is no significant difference between male teachers and female teachers in level of self confidence.

- There is no significant difference between male bank employees and female bank employees in level of self confidence.

METHOD

Participant

Total 200 professionals (teachers & bank employees) were randomly selected from various institutes of Sabarkantha district of Gujarat offering teaching and banking work profession, out of which 100 were from teachers and 100 were from banking work. Also sample separated in male and female. The sample was equally divided in regard to gender also.

Instruments

To identify the level of self confidence among the participants the Agnihotri's Self-Confidence Inventory (ASCI) was used. The ASCI has been developed by Dr. Rekha Gupta. The inventory consists 56 true-false type items and the lower the score the higher would the level of self confidence and vice-versa. The Split- Half reliability of the inventory is 0.91 and the level of validity of the ASCI with scores of Basavanna's (1975) Self-Confidence Inventory is 0.82.

Procedure

The permission for data collection was taken from the concerned authorities of the schools and bank office. The entire participants were approached at their place. They were told that the purpose of the data collection is only for a research and their responses would be used for research purposes only. The collected data was analyzed by Mean, SD and 't' test.

RESULTS AND DISCUSSION

As here pointed out previously that the prime aim of the study is to identify and compare the level of self confidence in professionals of teachers and bank employees. I also tried to find out differences separately between the group of male as well as female of teachers and bank employees. Here further we would like to mention that the score obtained on Agnihotri's Self-Confidence Inventory (ASCI) have its special meaning in contrast to generally interpretation of low and high score of a scale or inventory. In ASCI the lower the score the higher would the level of self confidence and vice-versa. The respondent or a group of respondent who score below 7 the interpretation would be that it has very high self confidence and in the same way the of 45 and above would be interpreted very low self confidence.

Here, state that the result in general reveals that the 't' value of the entire six table is found to be significant at 0.01 level.

Table: (1)

Showing Result of 't' test on Self Confidence with regard to Teachers v/s Bank Employees.

Variables	N	Mean	SD	't'	Significant
Teachers	100	21.38	2.83	9.88	0.01
Bank Employees	100	17.70	3.54		

*Significant level of 't' value: 0.05 level 1.97 (df=198), 0.01 level 2.60 (df=198)

As reported in Table. No.(1) bank employees exhibits lower mean score (M=17.70) then the teachers (M=21.33), it means bank employees demonstrate more self confidence than teacher, and 't' value of 9.88 clearly indicate that the differences between the two groups in self confidence level is find to be statistically significant at 0.01 level.

Table: (2)

Showing Result of 't' test on Self Confidence with regard to Male v/s Female.

Variables	N	Mean	SD	't'	Significant
Male	100	18.38	3.31	4.88	0.01
Female	100	20.65	3.68		

*Significant level of 't' value: 0.05 level 1.97 (df=198), 0.01 level 2.60 (df=198)

Table. No.(2) reveals results obtained by the group of male and female. As reported in Table. No.(2) male shows lower mean score (M=18.38) then the female ((M=20.65) and 't' value of 4.88 indicate that the differences between the two groups in self confidence level is find to be statistically significant at 0.01 level. Hence I can say that the male have high self confidence than female.

Table: (3)

Showing Result of 't' test on Self Confidence with regard to Male Teachers v/s Male Bank Employees.

Variables	N	Mean	SD	't'	Significant
Male Teachers	50	20.32	2.34	7.46	0.01
Male Bank Employees	50	16.44	3.00		

*Significant level of 't' value: 0.05 level 1.98 (df=98), 0.01 level 2.63 (df=98)

It is observe in Table. No.(3) that male bank employees shows lower mean score (M=16.44) then the male teachers ((M=20.32) and 't' value of 7.46 indicate that the differences between the two groups in self confidence level is find to be statistically significant at 0.01 level. Hence I can say that the male bank employees have high self confidence than male teachers.

Table: (4)

Showing Result of 't' test on Self Confidence with regard to Female Teachers v/s Female Bank Employees.

Variables	N	Mean	SD	't'	Significant
Female Teachers	50	22.34	2.93	6.48	0.01
Female Bank Employees	50	18.96	3.60		

*Significant level of 't' value: 0.05 level 1.98 (df=98), 0.01 level 2.63 (df=98)

Table. No.(4) reveals results obtained by the group of female teacher and female bank employees. As reported in Table. No.(4) male shows lower mean score (M=18.38) then the female ((M=20.65) and 't' value of 4.88 indicate that the differences between the two groups in self confidence level is find to be statistically significant at 0.01 level. Hence I can say that the male have high self confidence than female.

Table: (5)

Showing Result of 't' test on Self Confidence with regard to Male Teachers v/s Female Teachers.

Variables	N	Mean	SD	't'	Significant
Male Teachers	50	20.32	2.32	3.48	0.01
Female Teachers	50	22.34	2.93		

*Significant level of 't' value: 0.05 level 1.98 (df=98), 0.01 level 2.63 (df=98)

As reported in Table. No.(5) male teachers exhibits lower mean score (M=20.32) then the female teachers (M=22.34), it means male teachers demonstrate more self confidence than female teacher, and 't' value of 3.98 clearly indicate that the differences between the two groups in self confidence level is find to be statistically significant at 0.01 level.

Table: (6)

Showing Result of 't' test on Self Confidence with regard to Male Bank Employees v/s Female Bank Employees.

Variables	N	Mean	SD	't'	Significant
Male Bank Employees	50	16.44	3.00	3.45	0.01
Female Bank Employees	50	18.96	3.60		

*Significant level of 't' value: 0.05 level 1.98 (df=98), 0.01 level 2.63 (df=98)

It is observe in Table. No.(6) that male bank employees shows lower mean score (M=16.44) then the female bank employees ((M=18.96) and 't' value of 3.45 indicate that the differences between the two groups in self confidence level is find to be statistically significant at 0.01 level. Hence I can say that the male bank employees have high self confidence than female bank employees.

Conclusion

From the data available in Table Nos. 1 to 6 we easily come to conclusion that bank employees have high self confidence in compare to teachers. It may be in account of the competitive and clerical environment observe in bank office. The employees of bank may have more opportunity to prove their ability and groom their potentiality and hence it may be promote self confidence of their professional. Due to such environment the bank employees can develop and exhibit characteristic traits and behaviors listed by Dr. John M. Oldham (1995). While in our schools teachers who runs conventional courses and literature may not provide opportunity to develop the self confidence.

REFERENCES

- Basavanna, M.(1975). Manual for the Self Confidence Inventory, Rupa, Psychological Centre, Varanasi.

- Breckenridge, E.M; and Vincent, E.L.1965). Child Development, Philadelphia, Sauders.

- Gupta, R.(2005). Manual for the Agnihotri's Self-Confidence Inventory, (ASCI), National Psychological Corporation, Agra.

- Oldham, John M., and Lois B. Morris (1995).*The New Personality Self- Portrait: Why You Think, Work, Love, and Act the Way You Do.* Rev. ed. NewYork: Bantam.

6. Achievement Motivation and Human Development

Defined as the need to perform well or the striving for success, and evidenced by persistence and effort in the face of difficulties, achievement motivation is regarded as a central human motivation. Achievement contexts can be found anywhere—on the playing field, on stage, in an art studio, or even in a kitchen or a garden. To be sure, standards and even the definitions of success vary among contexts. Achievement Motivation – also referred to as the need for achievement, is an important determinant of aspiration, effort, and persistence when an individual expects his performance will be evaluated in relation to some standard of excellence. D. C. McClelland analyzed the achievement motivation in the children stories of different countries and compared it with the economic development of the countries. He writes that achievement motivation accounts for the rise of a country. He recommends investment in a man, not so much in a plan.

Achievement Motivation and Human Development

Achievement has always been prized by all societies. A great deal of emphasis has been placed on getting ahead, making something of oneself and obtaining recognition. Irrespective of the field of achievement, the great achievers, inventors and discoverers of the world have always been valued and honored for their enthusiasm, perseverance and contribution to the betterment of mankind. Modern man considers enterprise and success as the indices of esteem. One judges oneself and others by what one's achievements are, how they compare with those of others and how early in life one is able to attain them. Thus, today's society can rightly be termed as an achievement oriented one.

It has become very evident that success and achievement in life and learning too depend largely on how much one really wants to succeed and achieve and what cost in human effort and energy one is willing to bear, to reach the goal. In other words, motivation is said to account for one's success and achievement in life and determines one's extent of learning. Significant differences in the achievement of people with similar physical and cognitive abilities also highlight the fact that independent of ability; motivational factors exert a profound influence on a person's performance and achievement.

Thus, motivation has been identified as, the vital condition, the most powerful director of ail learning and achievement. It is also the factor that accounts for the variations in the achievement behavior of the same person at different times and the relatively permanent differences between people, in the goals they purse. Motivational factors also determine such critical things as whether people actually pursue and master skills that they are fully capable of mastering and they them- selves value.

Environmental influences specifically, caste, region, culture and socio-economic status as some of the determinant variables, play an important role in the formation of various social attitude, beliefs, values etc.

Today, the study of attitude remains one of the central concerns to the social researchers because attitudes play an important role in virtually to every aspect of social life. First they exert a powerful influence upon the nature of our relations with others. Attitudes influence most of our decisions. They determine our potions on many crucial issues and in this manner indirectly shape the nature of the society. Thus the formation of attitude is of great importance to the students of society, and of such great concern to the parents, educators, political leaders and all men who would teach or lead or control other men.

The prime aim of the research is to know about the development attitudes of the tribal area people. Moreover the investigator has attempted to see how the tribal culture and society affects on the attitudes of the development of the tribal area people.

People living on tribal belt have their own customs, conventions and beliefs in particular. They are living with their culture in society. The main aim of the study is to examine various attitudes of the tribal area people of North Gujarat as well as their attitudes towards educational, women, health, social, economic, industrial and infrastructure development.

Meaning of Development:

Before the birth of the 'Sociology of development', the focus of interest among social science mainly since world war II, began for the most part with economists and was phrased in terms of 'economic growth' or 'economic development.' Other social scientists become involved in conversation partly through economists and political scientists.

The meaning of development and or growth is not clear, confused, even in economics – a relatively science. Flamming (1997) has pointed out for us the confusion surrounding the terms 'economic growth' and 'economic development'. He has made a meticulous survey of the literature on the subject spreading over the past twenty years or so and come forward with the nine different senses in words 'development' and 'growth' have been used in economics.

There is no unanimity among the economists about their exact meaning. Meier frankly acknowledges that "It is difficult to give precise meaning to 'economic development; perhaps it is easier to say what 'economic development' is not". For a long time, there have been three major mechanical measures of growth for economists-gross national product, per capita income and per capita output.

Recently, scholars have enlarged the scope of economic development; it is defined as nothing less than the "upward movement of the entire social system, because in the final analysis" development is a human problems" (Myrdal-1953).

The economists have tried to make a distinction between development and growth. Meier (1966) notes; "Development is taken to mean growth plus change; there are essential qualitative dimensions in the development process that may be absent in the growth or expansion of an economy through a simple widening process."

There are two different major themes that the concept of development is used to convey in other social sciences. First, the development refers to a type of social change which originated in Europe beginning in the sixteen century. Here the analyses of social change have been mainly concerned with the forces which were responsible for the drastic social transformation out of a feudal social order. In this sense development come to stand for the contemporary transformation of "Traditional" or "Underdeveloped" countries in the direction of the economic and other structural features of highly developed western nations. Secondly, the development used for making comparison between developed and underdeveloped countries. Here in the scholar have been trying to spot out those features of underdeveloped societies which stand as barriers to development and pinpoint the missing structural characteristics in these societies which are found in the developed societies. Put differently, the term 'development' is used (1) to present the analysis of underdevelopment and suggest the measures of development of the developing society (Porter-1975) and (2) to present description of traditional, transitional and modern society in terms of economic development, including industrialization in the narrow sense of manufacturing, and wide ranging structural features that set developed societies apart from traditional or less developed ones. (Levy-1975)

Among the other social sciences which become mainly interested and involved in these problems are sociology, social psychology, anthropology and political science, among others. These social sciences draw ideas from all sources together in a common body of theory. There is, therefore, sufficient over planning. The best ideas, which emerged following the world war-II -a period of intense interest in development- are a mishmash of trivial. There is an outpouring of conflicting concepts.

These ideas had their root in European social economic and political philosophies and still lean towards the same.

The output of literature on economic and social development has in recent years reached massive proportions. But if one attempts to find from the context what definitions are implicit, one soon discovers that different and often conflicting concepts are being reflected by this term. One immediate confusion crops up from the relationship between economic and social development. For example, some scholars draw a distinction between economic and social development, some treat the two inseparable, and yet others leave the fate of social development exclusively to the economists. Penrose (1968) rightly observed: "It is of course common for economists to note the importance of (noneconomic) considerations, but usually only to ignore them". The other social sciences by contrast, "Illumine the social nature of economic development leaving economic development as such to economists." There is, thus, at tendency to define economic development to include the elements which neatly fall within the sphere of social development and to define social development which comes within the scope of economic development. In this manner they not only overlap but the analysis of social development as whole remains superficial and partial.

A close look at the literature dealing with the determinants of development reveals that there are two sets of theories regarding forces of change. One set of theories maintains that the forces of history originate from within human society, from its structure and culture. That is to say, the development is the result of internal, endogenous forces. As opposed to this, another set of theories regard society and its changes determined by forces originating outside the social system. In other words, the development is coursed by external, exogenous forces.

Some scholars play safer and pay attention to both depending upon their orientation and circumstances. Among these scholars, sometimes some discovers that there occurs economic development without social development, sometimes some perceive that there happens social development without economic development, and sometimes some find occurring both economic and social development.

Meaning of Achievement Motivation

Defined as the need to perform well or the striving for success, and evidenced by persistence and effort in the face of difficulties, achievement motivation is regarded as a central human motivation. Psychologist David McClelland (The Achieving Society, 1961) measured it by analyzing respondents' narratives; rather more controversially he hypothesized that it was related to economic growth. Lack of achievement motivation was, for a period during the 1950s and 1960s, a fashionable explanation for lack of economic development in the Third World—notably among certain American modernization theorists.

Atkinson (1964) states, "The theory of achievement motion attempts to account for the determinants of the direction, magnitude and persistence of behavior, in limited but very important domain of human activities.

In the words of Dave and Anand (1979) "Achievement Motivation is a desire to do well relative to some standard of excellence."

Colman, A.M. (2001) has defined achievement motivation as a social form of motivation involving a competitive desire to meet standards of excellence.

Thus, the basis of achievement motivation is achievement motive, i.e. motive to achieve. Those who engage themselves in a task account of an achievement motivation. Achievement motivation is expectancy of finding satisfaction in mastery of difficult and challenging performances where as in the field of education in particular it stands for the pursuit of excellence. Since need for achievement vary from one student to another, it may help in planning activities to know where students stands which students, for instance, have high achievement needs which are low in achievement and which seems primarily motivated by a need to avoid failure. Those who are more highly motivated to achieve are likely to respond well to challenging assignments, strict grading corrective feedback, new or unusual problems and the chance to try again. But, less challenging assignments, simple reinforcement for success, small steps for each task, lenient grading and protections from embarrassment are probably more successful strategies for those students who are very eager to avoid failure.

Achievement contexts can be found anywhere—on the playing field, on stage, in an art studio, or even in a kitchen or a garden. To be sure, standards and even the definitions of success vary among contexts. In sports success usually means winning, although it could also be defined in terms of personal improvement. Success for a pianist might be measured in the length of applause or in newspaper reviews, for a hostess in the amount of food the guests consume, and for a surgeon in patient survival rates. This article focuses primarily on school contexts, but most of the issues discussed apply to any context that involves some standard against which performance can be measured—any situation that offers the opportunity to succeed or fail.

David McClelland (believes that the need for achievement is a distinct human motive that can be distinguished from other needs. One characteristic of achievement motivated people is that they seem to be more concerned with personal achievement than with the rewards of success. He believes that they do not reject rewards but the rewards are not essential as the accomplishment itself. Atkinson theorized that orientation results from achieving success and avoiding failure. The motive to achieve success is determined by three things: (1) the need to succeed or need achievement (nAch); (2) the person's estimate of the likelihood of success in performing the particular task; and (3) the incentive for success-that is, how much the person wants to succeed in that particular task. The motive to avoid failure is determined by three similar considerations: (1) the need to avoid failure which, like the need to achieve success, (2) the person's estimate of the likelihood of failure at the particular task; and (3) the incentive value of failure at that task, that is, how unpleasant it would be to fail (Atkinson, 1966).

Both McClelland and Atkinson's achievement and motivation theory was based on a personality characteristic that manifested as a dispositional need to improve and perform well according to a certain standard of excellence In order to assess people's need for achievement, they used a projective instrument called the Thematic Appreciation Test (TAT) that elicits unconscious processes. In this instrument, people are asked to write a story describing the thoughts, emotions and behaviors of a person in an ambiguous picture or drawing (for example, a child sitting in front of a violin). The stories are then coded for achievement-related content including indicators of competition, accomplishments, and commitment to achieve. This technique, labeled the Picture Story Exercise (PSE), was used in numerous studies that tested the relations of nAch with various indicators of performance (Kaplan, 2509).

Achievement Motivation – also referred to as the need for achievement, is an important determinant of aspiration, effort, and persistence when an individual expects his performance will be evaluated in relation to some standard of excellence. Such behavior is called achievement-oriented.

Motivation – to achieve is instigates when an individual knows that he is responsible for the outcome of some venture, when he anticipates explicit knowledge of results that will define his success or failure, and when there is some degree of risk, i.e., some uncertainty about the outcome of his effort. The goal of achievement oriented activity is to succeed, to perform well in relation to a standard of excellence or in comparison with others who are competitors (McClelland 1961, Atkinson 1964).

Achievement – Achievement imagery in fantasy takes the form of thoughts about performing some task well, of sometimes being blocked, of trying various means of achieving, and of experiencing joy or sadness contingent upon the outcome of the effort. The particular diagnostic signs of achievement motivation were identified by experimental fact. The results of validating experiments have been replicated in other social groups and societies. Together these experimental findings specify what is counted in an imaginative protocol to yield the n Achievement source, an assessment of the strength of achievement motivation (McClelland et al. 1953, McClelland et al. 1958)

Achievement motivation is also affected by the parents' communication styles. Parents appear to be the primary influence on a child's motivation to learn (Wlodkowski & Jaynes, 1990). *Achievement motivation* is an important determinant of aspiration, effort and persistence when an individual expects that performance will be evaluated in relation to some standard of excellence (Atkinson & Birch, 1978). Achievement motivation drives an individual to excel, succeed, or outperform others at some task (Hockenbury & Hockenbury, 2503). Parental involvement improves academic performance and school behavior. It increases academic motivation, and decreases the number of dropouts (Flouri & Buchanan, 2503). When it comes to achievement, parents expect and evaluate attitudes of their own achievement. In addition, they communicate in different ways to pass on these evaluative attitudes to their children. Parents who support their children's ideas are related positively to achievement aspirations, and parents who give little feedback, and are uninvolved are negatively correlated with achievement aspirations. (Crandall, Katkovsky & Crandall, 1965).

Need for achievement (N-Ach) refers to an individual's desire for significant accomplishment, mastering of skills, control, or high standards. The term was first used by Henry Murray and associated with a range of actions. These include: "intense, prolonged and repeated efforts to accomplish something difficult. To work with singleness of purpose towards a high and distant goal. To have the determination to win". The concept of NAch was subsequently popularized by the psychologist David McClelland.

This personality trait is characterized by an enduring and consistent concern with setting and meeting high standards of achievement. This need is influenced by internal drive for action (intrinsic motivation), and the pressure exerted by the expectations of others (extrinsic motivation). Measured by thematic appreciation tests, need for achievement motivates an individual to succeed in competition, and to excel in activities important to him or her.

Need for Achievement is related to the difficulty of tasks people choose to undertake. Those with low N-Ach may choose very easy tasks, in order to minimize risk of failure, or highly difficult tasks, such that a failure would not be embarrassing. Those with high N-Ach tend to choose moderately difficult tasks, feeling that they are challenging, but within reach.

People high in N-Ach are characterized by a tendency to seek challenges and a high degree of independence. Their most satisfying reward is the recognition of their achievements. Sources of high N-Ach include:

1. Parents who encouraged independence in childhood
2. Praise and rewards for success
3. Association of achievement with positive feelings
4. Association of achievement with one's own competence and effort, not luck
5. A desire to be effective or challenged
6. Intrapersonal Strength
7. Desirability
8. Feasibility
9. Goal Setting Abilities.

For children who are not intrinsically motivated to engage in intellectual activities, intrinsic motivation theorists would determine first whether factors that research has shown to support intrinsic interest (e.g., feelings of control and competence) are present, and then manipulate those factors to increase interest (e.g., by providing students more autonomy or making sure they can succeed on tasks and feel competent).

While intrinsic motivation theorists emphasize feelings of enjoyment, self-worth theorists are concerned with feelings of being valued. Covington (1992, 1998) and others propose that students are naturally motivated to preserve a sense of personal worth. If a student believes his value in an educational context is based on academic competence, he will seek opportunities to demonstrate his competencies and, like Defensive Dave, avoid situations that may lead to a judgment of incompetence. Self-worth theorists, therefore, might assess students' beliefs about what others' regard is based on. Interventions might be aimed at making sure that students feel supported and admired for trying, regardless of the outcome of their efforts.

Related to self-worth theory, which emphasizes students' feelings of being valued, self-system theory claims that feeling socially connected is a basic human need and that people do not function well in environments where this need is not met. They study the quality of children's relationships with the teacher and classmates. They might suggest that a teacher make a greater effort to develop an emotionally close relationship with a child who is not exerting much effort. For example, a teacher or a counselor might reach out to Alienated Al to let him know that he or she cared about Al's academic success and is interested in understanding his feelings about school.

Achievement Motivation and Economic Development

D. C. McClelland analyzed the achievement motivation in the children stories of different countries and compared it with the economic development of the countries. The textbooks of certain countries mostly contained stories of success of active people. The textbooks of other countries contained stories of failure and misery. Twenty-five years later the economic development of the countries was analyzed. In the countries of the textbooks emphasizing success, the economic development had been positive, in the countries of negative-attitude textbooks, the economic gain was absent, or very insignificant. McClelland has drawn broad conclusions from his research findings. He writes that achievement motivation accounts for the rise of a country. He recommends investment in a man, not so much in a plan (McClelland, 1962).

After fifty years, we can conclude that the McClelland's study is an important part of social sciences. Many investigations are supporting its conclusions. R. L. Venecky (1992) has found a good harmony between achievement motivation in the textbooks and the number of patents in the USA in 1800-1960. R. Simon-Schaefer (1990) writes about an optimistic view on life in the Age of Enlightenment. Human understanding was considered boundless. The evolution theory taught that we are the best species of living beings. The optimistic view on life was interrelated with rapid economic and cultural development. M. M. Dubrovskaya (1992) has compared favored children stories in the USSR and the USA. In the first country, the characteristic hero was Ivanushka the Fool who lolled on the oven and waited until a princess came to marry him. In the second country, the most favored hero was Mickey Mouse. M. M. Dubrovskaya has told in her presentation that there was a clear relationship between the ethos of children stories and countries economic development.

D. C. McClelland has investigated the relationship of achievement motivation and economic development on the macro level. In this case, it is very difficult to reach the representatively of the subjects interviewed or the textbooks analyzed. Besides that, the used indices of economic development have been questioned by many critics. The relationship of achievement motivation and economic development is easier to investigate on the level of individual entrepreneurs. The investigators compare the personal characteristics of entrepreneurs with the success of their enterprises. Many studies of this kind have been made in the recent years. The results of the studies are supporting McClelland's idea.

D. L. Lee and E. W. K. Tsang (2001) have interviewed 168 entrepreneurs in Singapore. They have compared the growth rate of sales and the profit of the ventures with the need for achievement, internal locus of control, self-reliance, and the extroversion of the entrepreneurs. The need for Achievement was the personality trait which had the greatest impact on the venture performance (the path coefficient was 0.14 in PLS model).

M. Yasin (1996) has investigated the relationship in Arab culture. He has measured the entrepreneurial effectiveness by the annual income of the enterprises, the need for achievement by Job Choice Exercise, and the job satisfaction by the subject's responses to four questions. His subjects were 220 Jordanian entrepreneurs.

The culture of the previous text is that the high level of the need for achievement is important for economic development. We can say that it remains an important topic even nowadays. We can believe that achievement motivation facilitates development in other areas as well, for example, science, culture, etc.

Studies on Achievement Motivation

Research has shown there is an interest in Achievement Motivation as it relates to students. Many studies have been conducted to discover what motivates students (Atkinson, 1999; Atkinson and Feather, 1966; Spence, 1983). With these studies came ideas on how to predict an individual's task performance (Atkinson and Feather, 1966; Grabe, 1979; Mukherjee, 1964). Other studies have been conducted to increase student motivation. These studies also have spawned new ideas on motivation (Accordino, Accordino, & Slaney, 2000; Atkinson, E., 1999; Bar-Tal, Frieze, & Greenberg, 1974; Grabe, 1979; Latta, 1974; McClelland & Alschuler, 1971; Rathvon, 1999; Simons, Van Rheenen, & Covington, 1999; Veroff, 1975). This chapter will look at person's Need to Achieve, Fear of Failure, and Probability of Success at a task, Perception of the Outcome of a Task, and other testing methods.

One theory of Achievement Motivation was proposed by Atkinson and Feather (1966). They stated that a person's achievement oriented behavior is based on three parts: the first part being the individual's predisposition to achievement, the second part being the probability of success, and third, the individual's perception of value of the task. Atkinson and Feather (1966) state, "The strength of motivation to perform some act is assumed to be a multiplicative function of the strength of the motive, the expectancy (subjective probability) that the act will have as a consequence the attainment of an incentive, and the value of the incentive: Motivation = f(Motive X Expectancy X Incentive)" (p. 13).

The individual's perception of probability for achieving the task would cause a need to achieve and a fear of failure. Both are strong emotions that influence the individual's decision on whether or not to attempt the task (Bar-Tal, Frieze, and Greenberg, 1974). If a task simultaneously arouses an individual's motivation to approach the task and motivation to avoid the task, then the sum of the two motivations will be the result. If the result is more positive to approach the task, then the individual will be motivated toward the task. If the result is more positive to avoid the task, then the individual will be motivated to avoid the task. The strength of motivation also is important. Different variables are taken into account for each task. Often this is done subconsciously. These variables factor into how much the individual is motivated to approach or avoid the task (Atkinson and Feather, 1966). In a person motivated to achieve, their behavior is directed by a positive possibility. In a person motivated to avoid failure, their behavior is directed by an undesirable possibility. The same person may experience both motives at the same time depending on the situation. Which motive the person selects depends on the relative strength of the achievement motives, either to achieve success, or to avoid failure. An individual will find a task easy if they have a high probability of successfully completing the task. An individual will find a task hard if they have a low probability of successfully completing the task.

Successful people are confident, enthusiastic, and remain positive and optimistic. They expect to succeed. "Individuals with strong self – efficacy are less likely to give up than are those who are paralyzed with doubt about their capabilities" (Alderman, 1999, p. 60). Unsuccessful people often lack confidence and are negative and pessimistic, they rarely expect success. In fact, they expect to fail. "Everything that happens to you, everything you become and accomplish is determined by the way you think, by the way you use your mind" (Tracy, 1993, p. 59).

Our self-esteem and how competent we feel is what causes certain behaviors and establishes certain goals. Some people like to try new experiences and set more challenging goals, others prefer to stay in their comfort zones and be happy with what they know they can accomplish. But it is all based on our view of our self (Haasen and Shea, 1979).

Achievement Motivation and Development

S. P. Schatz (1965) wrote that the indices of economic development in McClelland's research were not representative and his data did not support his thesis. Twelve years later A. S. U. Mazur and Rosa E. (1977) used more advanced methods for the analysis of McClelland's data for the years 1950 -1971 and found no correlation between the achievement motivation of nations and their economic development in the following years. C. J. Gilleard (1989) correlated recent data of economic development of 34 countries in the years 1950-1977 and the data about achievement motivation in 1950 from McClelland's study. He found no correlation. In 1961 McClelland prognosticated that certain countries would be more successful than others. The prognostication proved not correct in 1989 at least for some countries. C. J. Gilleard (1989) concludes that he could not find any support to McClelland's theory that achievement motivation influences national economic growth. He admits that there can be correlation between the economic success of a person and its level of achievement motivation. No one of McClelland's critics has reanalyzed his data from 1925.

The critics have paid attention to the measures of economic development; however, the deficiencies can be in the measures of achievement motivation as well. It was mentioned above that the measures of economic development were not representative in some cases. Were the measures of achievement motivation representative? Was the sample of the analyzed textbooks and children story books representative to all the books available for children at this time in this country? Were the persons interviewed in measuring the nation's level of achievement motivation representative of the nation's active population? If the samples of interviewed persons or analyzed textbooks are described in the papers then reader can conclude that the samples were not representative.

The different measures of achievement motivation do not correlate with each other and are not very reliable. M. Yasin (1996) accepts the conclusion of B. R. Johnson that the achievement measurement instruments are unreliable. J. Collins, P. J. Hanges and E. A. Locke (2004, 98) wrote that the reliability of TAT is often less than .60. The two important instruments for the measurement of achievement motivation - TAT and Lynn's Achievement Motivation scale, had a negative correlation in J. Langan-Fox (1995) study. J. Collins, P. J. Hanges and E. A. Locke (2004, 112) also conclude that TAT and the questionnaire measures do not correlate with each other but both of them are valid measures of achievement motivation. The validity can be explained in this case by the assumption that achievement motivation is not a very clear concept and it has different aspects. The investigated aspects of achievement motivation are even independent from each other. If we accept that there is one concept of achievement motivation, then the factor analysis of its different measures might clear up the best measures of achievement motivation or the best combination of the measures.

D. C. McClelland has investigated the relationship of achievement motivation and economic development on the macro level. In this case, it is very difficult to reach the representatively of the subjects interviewed or the textbooks analyzed. Besides that, the used indices of economic development have been questioned by many critics. The relationship of achievement motivation and economic development is easier to investigate on the level of individual entrepreneurs. The investigators compare the personal characteristics of entrepreneurs with the success of their enterprises. Many studies of this kind have been made in the recent years. The results of the studies are supporting McClelland's idea.

D. L. Lee and E. W. K. Tsang (2001) have interviewed 168 entrepreneurs in Singapore. They have compared the growth rate of sales and the profit of the ventures with the need for achievement, internal locus of control, self-reliance, and the extroversion of the entrepreneurs. The need for Achievement was the personality trait which had the greatest impact on the venture performance (the path coefficient was 0.14 in PLS model). An analogical research was carried out by F. W. Swierczek and T. than Ha (2003) in Vietnam. They also found that SME owners were motivated by challenge and achievement.

M. Yasin (1996) has investigated the relationship in Arab culture. He has measured the entrepreneurial effectiveness by the annual income of the enterprises, the need for achievement by Job Choice Exercise, and the job satisfaction by the subject's responses to four questions. His subjects were 220 Jordanian entrepreneurs. M. Yasin has found positive and rather high correlations between the three measures. For example, the correlation between the need for achievement and job satisfaction was .66. The need of achievement added .17 to the quadrate of the coefficient of multiple correlations in the regression model of income.

F. Diaz and A. Rodrigues (2003) have studied 38 entrepreneurs from Andalusian cooperatives. They measured the locus of control by the Rotter Scale and the need of achievement by the Lynn's Achievement Motivation Questionnaire. They compared the average results with the norms for population in general and with the average data for entrepreneurs from small and medium-size companies. F. Diaz and A. Rodriguez conclude that the achievement motivation and the locus of control of entrepreneurs from cooperatives are halfway between the SME entrepreneurs and the qualified workers.

K. i. Suzuki, S.-H. Kim, and Z.-T Bae (2002) made an interesting comparison of entrepreneurs in two countries. They conducted a survey of 396 Japanese firms and 188 Silicon Valley firms. In both countries, entrepreneurial motivation was important - entrepreneurs pursued their challenge in life and sought to improve their capabilities. The entrepreneurs in Japan valued social recognition higher than the entrepreneurs in the Silicon Valley. The latter paid more attention to a better quality of life and making money. Entrepreneurs in both countries considered competitors, lack of funds and poor sales as influential risks. Japanese entrepreneurs paid more attention to technical, human, and organisational risks. Entrepreneurs in the Silicon Valley were more concerned with marketing and financial risks. We see that social factors constitute a more important component of entrepreneurial motivation in Japan and financial factors in the Silicon Valley.

The achievement motivation has been proven to be important for venture growth in different cultures. However, the relationship of Confucian ethics to entrepreneurship is not very clear. The "Five Dragons" in the Asia-Pacific region (Japan, Taiwan, South Korea, Hong Kong, and Singapore) have very high rates of economic growth but the Superior Man in Confucian ethics thinks about righteousness not about gain. T. C. Hsiao (1997) composed a questionnaire for 395 R&D professionals in Taiwan. The questions were aimed at finding out the R&D professional type according to Confucian standards. The Superior Man thinks about law and behaves according to the law. He is affable and satisfied. The Superior man is aimed at developing himself. The Inferior man thinks about his personal benefits and he is always distressed. He is adulatory and seeks the other people to do what he wants. The children are taught to be the Superior Man. T. C. Hsiao has found that the Superior Man type R&D workers are mostly engaged in technical staff work and the Inferior Man type R&D workers are mostly engaged in managerial work. He concludes that the Confucian value system is quite unfavourable for the management. T. C. Hsiao (1997) compares the two leaders of China: Chiang Kai-shek and Mao Tse-tung. Chiang Kai-shek was a Superior Man and Mao Tse-tung an Inferior Man. Under the leadership of Chiang Kai-shek, Taiwan's economy achieved marvelous results. We see the validity of the Weber's idea: a successful businessman has to be honest. It is time to transfer the principle to politicians as well.

The ethos of the previous text is that the high level of the need for achievement is important for economic development. At the same time, S. Singh (1977) writes (relying on S. A. Rudin's research) that nations with a high need for achievement may have a high death rate from hypertension and other illnesses. J. Langan-Fox (1995) has found that the entrepreneurs with a very high level of need for achievement were the lowest in job satisfaction. She writes that the persons are all the time aspiring the very high standards of excellence and can never be satisfied. There should be an optimal level of the need for achievement.

In this regard, the investigation by B. D. Kirkcaldy, A. Furnham, and T. Martin (1998) is very interesting. The authors have compared attitudinal variables, economic variables and the subjective well-being of 14,188 subjects in 53 countries. Some of the attitudinal variables were defined as follows. Competitiveness is the motive to outperform other persons. Mastery is the need to master problems and situations. Achievement conformity is the commitment to the organisation and its success. The values of subjective well-being for the 53 nations were taken from the research of E. Diener, M. Diener, and C. Deaner from 1995. The regression analysis of the data revealed that the subjective well-being of nations could be explained by four attitudinal variables: high mastery, low competitiveness, high achievement conformity, and low importance attached to money. "individuals with instrumental beliefs and commitments as well as achievement orientation, but who are cooperative and not exclusively materially oriented, have higher well-being" (Kirkcaldy, Furnham, and Martin, 1998, p 260). The highest level of achievement motivation is not the best. In another research, B. D. Kirkcaldy, A. Furnham, and R. Levine (2001) explain that competitiveness and work ethics are important for the development of a country at the early stages of industrialisation. The indices are not any more important when the plateau of development has been achieved. Cooperation is important for the well-being at this level of development and it fosters economic development as well.

Even more interesting was the curvilinear relationship between the quality of life (HDI) and competitiveness in the research by B. D. Kirkcaldy, A. Furnham, and T. Martin (1998). The overall correlation between the variables is negative. The higher the competitiveness, the lower the quality of life. But competitiveness is a part of achievement motivation. When competitiveness is low, then ascending competitiveness accompanies the ascending of the quality of life. However, very soon the further raising of competitiveness leads to the decline in the quality of life. The need for achievement should not be the only driving force of people.

To conclude the exciting overview about the achievement motivation and economic development, we can say that it remains an important topic even nowadays. Despite the fact that the severe critics addressed the different aspects of the investigations on the macro level, in recent years we can find many investigations on the micro level supporting the idea that high achievement motivation coincides with the rapid development of enterprises. We can believe that achievement motivation facilitates development in other areas as well, for example, science, culture, etc.

One fundamental lack and perspective of the investigations is to be mentioned. Almost all of the investigations rely on the correlation and not the causal relationship. The idea of the investigations carried out is as follows. Two or more groups of people (countries, firms) are compared on the level of achievement motivation and economic development. Usually the group with a higher economic development has the higher level of achievement motivation as well. However, the data do not reveal which of the two indicators is the cause and which is the effect. May be the high level of achievement motivation has facilitated economic growth. It may also be that the high economic level has raised the level of achievement motivation. There can be even a third indicator that causes the raise in both investigated indices. For example, the habit to work hard may raise the achievement motivation and develop economy. An analogical situation characterizes textbook research: the familiarity of a topic in society enables the author of texts to use simple sentences and known words and at the same time students have more correct answers to the questions from familiar topics.

Is the high level of achievement motivation a cause of rapid economic development, as we believe? To have a firmly based answer, we need the investigations of causal relationship. In a causal investigation, the achievement motivation of a group of people will be raised by educational means and then the economic success of the group in the following years will be compared with the economic success of a comparable group that did not receive the educational treatment. O. C. Hansemark (2003) has recently made such a small research and found that people from the experimental group were establishing enterprises more often in the following years than the people from the non-treated group. M. Yasin (1996, 75) also believes that the investment in achievement training may be significant for economic growth.

REFERENCES

1) **Atkinson, J. W., & Birch, D. (1978)**: An Introduction to Motivation. New York: D. Van Nostrand Company.

2) **Campbell, D.E., & Beets, J.L. (1977):** Meteorological variables and behavior: An annotated bibliography. FSS Catalog of Selected Documents in psychology, 7,1 (Ms. No. 1403).

3) **Campbell, D.T. (1950):** The indirect assessment of social attitudes. Psychological Bulletin, 47, 15-38.

4) **D. C. McClelland. (1961)**: The Achieving Society. Free Press, New York

5) **D.D. Nag, Baiga. (1958):** Economy of Madhya Pradesh, M.K. Publications, Calcutta.

6) **Gilleard C. J. (1989):** The achieving society revisited: A further analysis of the relation between national economic growth and need achievement. Journal of Economic Psychology, Vol. 10, Issue 1, p21, 13 p.

7) **L.P Vidyarthi, (1970):** Socio-cultural Implication of Industrialization in India, Planning Commission, New Delhi.

8) **McClelland D. C. (1962):** Business drive and national development. Harvard Business Review, Vol. 40, Issue 4, p99, 14 p.

9) **McClelland, D.C., Atkinson, J.W., Clark, P.W.S. and Lowell, E.C. (1953):** The Achievement Motive, New York: Appelenton-Century Crofts.

10) **Meier (1966):** The meaning of Economic Development. In Libera: R.W.Clower et al. Growth without Development Evanston.

11) **Singh S. (1977):** Achievement motivation and economic growth. Indian Psychological Review, Vol. 14, No 3, pp. 52 -56.

12) **Vimal Shah,(1969):** Tribal Economy in Gujarat, Well Print Publications, Jaipur.

www.ingramcontent.com/pod-product-compliance
Lightning Source LLC
Chambersburg PA
CBHW071059280326
41928CB00050B/2560